# How to Kill a Player!

## Exposing the Game

*by*

*Traci Gaines*

Bloomington, IN  Milton Keynes, UK

authorHOUSE®

and that is how I got the information for this book. I would also like to thank my enemies, the ex's, the players, and the bachelors because without them, I would not have learned from my mistakes or my inspirations. Whatever hurts you makes you stronger!!!! Whatever helps you, makes you a better person!!! You learn something new everyday, and you must add that to the intellegence that you already possess!!!

# Table of Topics

15. Women will do anything for a player.

16. Interest between the two people.

17. Playing and communication.

18. Women being ho's!Please!

19. Player is done with you for sex!

20. The internet is full of sex and sexual situations!

These are just a few of the topics that are inside, you'll have to finish reading just to see what else I have in store for the masses. There are a lot of things that are going on in this world of ours that we women must be aware of. Most of it we already know but I wanted to write down some of the secrets that I knew, to let the world know what's going on!

# Foreward by Traci Gaines

9/16/03

<u>How to Kill A Player</u>

When I first decided to write this novel I wanted to call it the s gene.  The s stood for stupid,with which I came up with a new definition for that.  This definition, I came up with on 10-15-01.  Stupid-Severely teched(touched) with an unknown sense of pride,instability or(inability), and dependence(dependency).

The s gene has some topics that I will choose to write on in time.  The first topic is women in love.  The second is why men have sex with women.  The third is having self esteem. The fourth is having confidence. The next is the mother instinct. The next is alcohol and the effects of it.  The next topic is why go back.  The next is the rewards of being self confident.  the last is why men treat women the way they do.

Now I have decided to call the book How to kill a player. I've been writing day by day and have talked with a lot of people about their relationships and what they think of women or men, for that matter.  So I have decided to make up my mind and expose the world to my point of view of why men are players and the women who love them, or don't.

# Introduction

This book is for the women that I feel have been stepped on, beaten up, or torchered by men. I say that because women go through a lot with men. They have to deal with their attitudes. They have to deal with their way of living, be it clean or messy. They have to deal with their cheating and playing around, and then they get to work on themselves. I thought when I wrote the book that I had written for the more naive women. I know that a lot of women out there won't even put up with most of the things I say in this book. To me women are not stupid, we just have that mother instinct in us, or the sympathetic gene, that is instilled in our bodies. I know that women wear many hats, and can accomplish all kinds of things. I also know about men, from just talking to them you can find out a lot about their lives. The things that you don't know, they would die first before telling you. There are some things though, if you watched c losely and paid real good attention, you can see what's going on behind the, c urtain so to speak. Some women may get offended by what they read in this book. Some women may appreciate it. Some women may get offended by the language used in this book,too. But think back when you were teenagers. You were taught by your mother not to curse or do bad things, but most teenagers do what they want when their not at home. The education system is a good example, it's not that the parents haven't taught the children the rules, but when the parents are not around they do a lot of things they aren't supposed to. The same is true for adults,we may act like angels but behind c losed doors,boy I could tell you some stories. I feel that all women should tell who their man is, only because that way we would no if our men were cheating. I feel that we should have more marriages because we could work together as a team, start or own businesses, and make a good living for ourselves. I also feel that if a woman is in a dangerous situation, find a shelter don't just put up with getting beat. Seriously, just call the police to get help. You can start over again, get three jobs to provide for yourself. There are definitely better men out there, and you guys can take care of each other. A lot of women go through molestation, rape, alcoholism, drug addiction, prostitution, and a lot of other detrimental situations. This book is just a stepping stone for me. I will have a lot more books that I will write to give other view points about life and how I feel about it. I have also talked to other women about the men that they have had to deal with and that is also why I decided to write this book. We go through a lot in life, let alone having to try and make our lives better. This is just my point of view and I have finally put it on paper it is a great release. I know that I was once told people, that when I finally matured that I would not put up with so much. I know that I have met women older than me, even when I was a teenager, that was going through some of the situations that I have mentioned in this book. Some of the situations in this book I have been going through since I was a teenager. I may not be a renown psychiatrist, but I have talked and listened to many women and men about their relationships and what they're going through. The reason I say that marraige would work better is because for the childrens sake. I belive that some, or maybe even most of us, would benefit better from their parents staying together. There are a lot of baby's mamas out there. I don't think it's because they all felt that they could raise their children on their own. I believe, there are some men who get a lot of women pregnant and then go back to them to sleep with them, or stay with them for a little while. They try to not have to pay child support, or get money from them. This is why I call myself a single woman and have cut all ties with most men. I only need one man in my life, which is the way I'm sure most women feel. There are some women who may feel that they don't need a man. They may feel that they don't want to get tied down right now. There are a whole lot of things that women and men go through, and this is my story.

# *How To Kill A Player!!!!!*

There are a lot of men out in this great big world of ours that are players. You have the bachelor who needs to have love from more than one female, sometimes three or four at a time. You have the married player who states that he is married but that his wife is a bitch or doesn't take care of the children, goes out to party too much,etc. You have the baby's mama player that has a baby's mama, but claims that he's not married yet, so that they can continue to see one other, or more women so that he doesn't have to commit. Then there is the forward player that says he has a woman or two and can play around with more women. Also his woman states that she knows her man is a player and it's almost as if she's boasting about it.

I had a conversation with two men that I know. They stated that most women look for dogs. They say that some women also look for men that are on drugs, or when they find out that their men are on drugs they ignore what's going on, and stick to his side. They stated that a man can be right in thier face that has a job,place to stay, and is a good man. She will not pay any attention to him.

I was asked questions about the men that I have dealt with in the past. I mentioned that with my high school sweetheart, he got involved with me, but he had a girlfriend at the time. He left her for me. I also spoke sbout an ex of mine that worked with computers, but he quit one job, and was drinking a lot. We were together for 5 years. Also there was a different ex that I had, and still has a baby's mama. He states that he doesn't want his son to go without his mother and father being together. He also is a stalker. We would fall out because of all his lies, then he would call again asking how the family is and can we make it to his block party.

I have also had the pleasure of being around men when they are pursuing other females. One day you'll see them with their wives, the next evening you'll see them talking to, or trying to take to a motel, another woman. There have also been instances where I have been the other woman. I have had calls from girls saying that they found my number in their mans' pocket and they called me to see where I had met him, and what was he doing or saying to me. Also, they wondered if he had mentioned that he had a girlfriend.

Also with the 2 men I spoke with,they mentioned that women were on womens lib and were spending money on men. They mentioned that all they had to do was be there to support a woman. I mentioned to my man, that men are now out here looking for the highest bidder.

I also wanted to touch on the side of the relationship, where you can still have friends male or female. I know some people who are married and still date. They say that they are not doing anything wrong because their spouse trusts them and understands.

There are also players now a days, as we say, that literally just come out and say lets have sex. I spoke with one guy and he has a very prominent job, condo, and is handsome. He states that some married women are just looking for a one night stand, then go home to hubby. I know myself, there are some women who only want one night stands. They don't want to commit,they just want to sleep with one guy, maybe once or on a constant basis instead of being committed.

I was told about women who get the same man,one right after the other. It's like they ignore the signs. I've also been told not to look for a man,that he will come to you. I know for all my life I never asked or looked for a man, they come to me, and if they are mostly dogs then I can't help, that. Look how they greet each other,what's up dog! I just look every man in the face when they do that. Are they supposed to be respected by that name? Does that make them more macho? Will they respond by saying oh,that's just how we greet each other?

I know when I'm in a bar or with a guy in general and a guy will whisper, "Is that you?"I don't know if they mean girlfriend,or sexpartner, or will they try for the girl if she's not with him. Let me tell you from experiences some do ask,right after they  hear the answer,they'll say their name,intrtoduce themselves, or use a pickup line. All the pick up lines that I've heard in years, I should have written down, some women would be familiar with them.

I know there are men out there that would have women to move with them and then beat them because the women didn't have money, or just wouldn't get a job. I know men that would move in with a women so he could steal her blind. I know men who would stay with a woman so that he could have a place to stay so that he didn't have to pay the rent.

Threre are men who also want and c rave phone sex. There were a few men that I came in c ontact with that would try to talk about sex on the phone, even in between "a normal", c onversation. I've been told about some men while having phone sex who want to have sex with their daughters.

There are men who have been molested or abused when they were little. Not all of them react to their c hildhood violently. Some choose to keep their past the past, and move on to their future.

There are guys that I know that will talk on their cell phones while outside. There is an ex of mine that would talk to me while his baby's mama was in the house with his son.

Some guys also have the star struck syndrome, where they like to see a women of their dreams. She could be a singer, sports star, or in a news broadcast. I wonder if it's because of wanting someone they can't have.

There are men who use music to woo their women. There are a lot of love songs that send a women into submission. A lot of the songs really pertain to the love,pain,hurt, and confusion that people go through while being in a relationship.

Alcohol can effect some men in a violent way. There may be a problem with a lot of men, for some reason they tend to fight their girlfriends, or each other.

Some men c laim that they wil help a woman out with money. They say that they haven't gotten paid yet,so they can't help you when you ask for it. Then they also don't call you, to tell you that they don't have the money anymore. There are however some men who actually help you out when you ask for it. The main thing is to get yourself together, so that you don't have to depend on the man in your life. There are also the good men who help you with whatever amount of money you need, and to them I give mucho mucho bueno, very very good,props. Along with the men that give gifts every now and then.

The way to make a realtionship fresh again men, is to give your friend, or girlfriend gifts. The way to a girls heart is to give her a gift. Some flowers,perfume, or shoes can make a girl overjoyed. Women always love to recieve gifts from her man.

The first part of the relationship is the I can give you anything stage, which most people give each other things to impress the other. After the relationship is new, you don't give each other things anymore. I suppose it changes to holidays, or birthdays. Most men don't try to give anything on birthdays or holidays, they just try to rec ieve.

There are a lot of things you would do for a man. Women go through leaps and bounds. I was once told a camel will go far to find water. There are a lot of things that guys do for women also. I've had some c heap ones to give like doughnuts and flowers. But I spent 5 years with the person. We used to be around each other all the time. He really cared for me but I wasn't really for marriage. I guess it tells the truth of settling down when the time is right between the two people.

There must be a c ertain amount of interest between you and the person. One time, I had so much in common with one guy it scared us and drove us apart. We talked, it even got to where we finished each others sentence, before it ended or began.

It is hard to deal with the playing that goes on in a relationship. The only way you can deal with it, is to talk about it with your partner. No matter whether you are playing or are serious, you should talk over good and bad things.

Women are looked at as objects. They are known as"tits and ass". Being intimate with your partner is a very sensitive subject. Sometimes a womens sexual appetite can be taken the wrong way. Each women is different, as far as how often they engage in sex with thier man, or male friend.

I am really p o'd about this ho mentality, that guys have about women. Guys say that women are fast. A guy will tell you anything to get in your pants. A women is a ho because she sleeps with more than one man. I don't mean one after the other,I'm talking about a women in a relationship for 3 months, then turns around and gets into another one. You know, I have to say that some guys just sleep with you as many times as you let them, then when their tired they push you away. They will also throw you to the curb if you pitch too much. If you mention the word marriage, or that you can't be with them and other men. I understand how a man has to be a man and sleep with other women,but is there a point when he settles down

8

and doesn't do that anymore?  Is there a difference when you just know that your man isn't cheating,when he really is?  From what I've been told,men think about sex 24/7.  I know for myself I usually can get off at least once a day.

I guess my next reasearch will be on how many times a guy really thinks about sex.  I've spoke to a man that says on a good day he can go for it 4 times a day.  On a bad day It's 3 times.  I remember when I was in my younger years, my friend and I used to count, it was about seven times a day.  Like they used to say f...ing like rabbits.  I've heard on talk shows where a guy has thirty-five women.  I know in my phone book alone I have 85 numbers of guys,just meeting them at the bars, or on the job.  I'm not counting just business associates or students from college.  I also didn't include the numbers that I've recieved over the years that were handed to me on a napkin, or small peace of paper,that I eventually lost.

When it comes to you asking a guy for some(sex) after he's used you, he will tell you no.  I've just been told no twice in one night.  I used an experiment, I asked them to be intimate with me and they both told me no, but as long as I gave in, when they asked for it, they took it.  One guy even got upset because I told him no, when he asked me for oral sex.

All this means is that you need to wait and look long and hard at the mate you are going to choose. Men will use you for your c oochie as long as you let them. For most men, now it seems, that if you do it on the first time, meaning night, day, or a few days there after, they won't repect you. If you wait from 5 months to a year, they still will not respect you, and watchout! They may still only want one thing! There is a friend of mine that waited 8 months for a girl, had sex, and then left her.

The internet is another way for players to play their games. Men email you or send bad pictures of themselves in compromising positions. To me this is very vulgar. For other people it might be pleasurable. I guess that's why people warn you about being on the internet and about being in those kinds of situations. The internet, of course, is a great way to get information through many other positive sources.

It's amazing how powerful a woman can be by not having intercourse. I've spoke to many women who say that you get more respect by using abstinance. If you look around and observe, you'll see that you get more attention when you don't give in so easily. I know that temptation is hard. I've also heard that some people get addicted to sex.

There is a friend, that I heard say, a guy that he knows has six women that are giving him money and taking care of him. There is another man that said he has four sugar mama's. I mentioned to him that I felt a man is not a real man if he's taking money from a woman. To me a real man is a man that either takes care of his woman, or helps her out every now and then. I feel that in a relationship two people should be equal, not one doing more for the other. If a man can take care of his woman totally, to me he is a great man. I know I had a   conversation with a man about this subject and he said that I was looking for a sucker. I told him no, that I was looking for a real man, not a boy or a player. It seems to me that the word player is truely the word "pimp" in disguise. I don't think this is fair to women. It's not our fault that we can work at certain places of employment, and keep a job. If you look at it we go through all the hard work and keep the job.

I believe that some men ration out the money to only a few of the women that they have, then they ration out sex so that the women will be intrigued and trapped by the drama. You fight because you don't have enough money. Then you fight because your not having enough sex, then you make up. It's a back and forth situation.

It's been four months now with a player that I've been with. If I go back and forth with him, it could go on forever. he probably only bothers to spend time with me because i have money, or may go to bed with him. I'm not interested in any of it now. I want a committment and I want to get married. I will find a good man one day.

I must add also that older men have told me that they help women with money, or what they need. I also know that with some oldermen that help comes with the price of sex in return. I know that most women will only put up with so much.

I know there are women out there that know the game or mastery of getting money or gifts from men without having to give up their bodies in return.

I have spoken with a lot of women who want to get married. There are women who have told me that after 4 or 5 years they must get married to thier man or their leaving them. I know there are some women who will not put up with their men only giving them a little bit of money. There some women that say their man is a dog and their ok with that. Then they say if their man brings them the money their ok with it.

I've always known that their were women who get men to buy their jewelry, c lothes, houses, take them on trips, etc. These are the women that I need to talk to next to see how they accomplish this. I've often wondered if men do this for the women because they already have something going for themselves. I know a women that was a psychiatrist and she said that men treated her all the time. There is a guy that I used to know, his girl friend, was a nurse with 2 girls. They were going to get married,they've been married for 3 4 years now. There is a guy that is now a vice principal. He is married with a son and his wife doesn't work. They've been married for about 3 years. Then there are couples who have been married for ten years and up. I talked to a medical assistant, she and her husband have been married for ten years and they were high school sweethearts.

I still wonder if some men only want to a marry a woman without kids. I know that some men require things for women too,like they must cook, she can't drink,etc. Women and men have lists for the qualifications of a mate.

Women should beware of the men that have friends. I feel either they tell each other "Oh yeah, you can get at her, she doesn't mean anything to me". Or they may just try to talk to the women any way. I witnessed a situation where a guys friend flirted with a women. She said that he had never approached her before. Then her man called on her cell phone and said he was on his way to the c lub. When he came they went outside, he and the women, to talk. When she came back in she was crying and then they left. I tried to tell her that it wasn't worth it but she stayed in their a little while longer, and now he's gone. She was giving him money to help out also, then she stopped, but I tried to warn her to watch out for that too.

They are like lions or snakes, they will sit and wait until your ready. Then they'll slither or pounce for the kill. I still feel as long as you have something they can USE, they will keep you by their side.

The phone calls over the years have made me upset for a long time. Most of the time when a man says,"I'll call you",It's not true. it's just to keep you trapped in the house by the phone waiting. So that no other man can approach, also. The other reason is to see what you are doing, so they'll know if they have to go to a different c lub. "I'll call you", also means let me call some of the other women first to see if they have a better offer, or something better to do or use. The other phone call is the phone call while the other women is in the house. The guy will sit up there and go yes ,uh huh, or something like that. Their just answering the other womans comments. Don't forget they call other women man too.

I don't believe that a man should be able to not have a job and live off of a woman. If a man doesn't have the skills to get an education, then learn a trade. I read a book on how to get rich and the man said go to college to study business, then

14

open your own business. For a man to be able to sit at home and do nothing but watch tv until his wife comes home, makes me sick. If you are weak in some areas, read a book to learn the skill, if you don't want to go to college.

There are some men who ask you to go out to dinner or to a movie, but it has to be some where, where no one he knows will see you and him together. They will inc lude alcohol or lots of food if you want it, but it's so they can feel on you now, or have sex with you later. Then the women feel guilty because she's been treated out, but if you think about it, that's not a lot. He didn't spend a lot of money, only a little, and it's like getting paid for sex with a little extra bonus.

There are some men who don't want to be seen with you in public. I know it's because they don't want their other women to see you with them. Also, they don't want the other women to think that their spending any money. How can they get help if they're spending some money on you?

There are some men who will not stop calling after they have stopped seeing you. They will either call once a week to try to get you to change your mind, or they will call once a year. I feel that they have gone through all the women that they could. They have figured out that you are a good woman and have tried to call to get you back. I also feel that there may be a group dec ision with men that if a woman doesn't ever get married that she's desperate. There is also the fact that a man will try to mess with a woman even if she's married. The first question they ask is ,"is it going ok?" I've been told by men that married and big women give it up very easily.

There are men who try to get women who are fast. I always ask men do they know the women's past. I ask has she been molested, or raped. The men ususally talk very, very badly about the women. The women are thinking,"Oh they like me, or my stuff is so good that he must love me." The men also sweet talk the women so much. They lie to get you into their trap. They tell you you're beautiful. They tell you they have a great job. They will give you positive feedback about yourself. Some men love to talk mean to a woman, to break down her self esteem, so that they won't mess with anyone else. Truthfully, their is always a better man out there than the one you are with. To find a good one it may take a long, long time. Just hold on until he comes your way. A woman has told me that it has taken her 19 years to find a good one, and he is a sweetheart.

There are some men who will only mess with a younger woman. To me this is because a younger woman, will almost believe everything you tell her. Some men say that younger girls or women are just freaky. I feel that they're looking for a father figure, so they deal with an older man. They feel that sex is good, or may possibly even be addicted to it. They don't care about getting diseases. When drugs or alcohol are involved, they cannot think straight. Once the situation is over they either forget what happened, they go back for more, or they try to stop dealing with the guy. Believe me, these men can't be trusted. They will talk so sweet to you, buy you things, or just look at you in a sympathetic way. You've gotta be careful about the game. You need to keep on your toes so that the men will respect you.

There are men out there that will not respect you if you go to bed with them too soon. Some men will say to them that it doesn't matter, but that's not true. Again they are just telling you what you want to hear. Most of the time they don't care about having a relationship with you. They just want to go to bed with you more than once. They may only sleep with you until you get pregnant. I was told by an ex of mine that his uncle told him all he had to do was get a girl pregnant, he would be able to sleep with her for the rest of her life. They may sleep with you for up to 2 or 3 years. It just depends on what you want to deal with. It also depends on what you want in life, like marriage, long term partnership only, or whatever the case may be.

What do you do when you find artic les in the house? Some men may have condoms, earrings, c lothes, etc. in the house. Most likely if there are womens' c lothes there is a woman staying with them. They will try to c laim that it's their sisters, cousins, or mothers' clothing. An ex of mine would not let me leave anything in the house, because of the next woman. Another would let me leave stuff but would cover it up. I figured he was covering up my stuff for the next woman.

There are some men who will let you spend the night. I believe it's because the woman must work graveyard shift, or it's not the right time to stay over. Maybe the woman has two jobs, or she is on vacation. To me that's the main reason that men don't marry the woman, that way they can pick and choose who and where they want to spend the night or to satisfy their hunger.

There are some men who will pay for women to go to a hotel. They will spend from the c heapest amount all the way up to the more expensive ones. What they are trying to do is just get their fix for the night. Yes, you may do something that their woman doesn't do, but she doesn't do it everyday for a reason. I used to think that if a guy held out from giving me sex that he was tired from being with another woman. That maybe true, but it is wonderful that a guy can just lay down with you and not have sex all the time. I know a guy that would say that he couldn't just lay down with a woman without having sex. That was a lie, he could lay still with his woman but not me.

There are some men that think that their mid-sections are Gods' gift to women. They think that they can intice, or hold a woman at bay just with their lower head, as we used to say. Some men think they are big or that size doesn't matter. Size does matter and women talk about it all the time. I know I couldn't tell a guy that he is too small, but I will say that if women keep leaving you, there may be a problem. Also, if you need to get bigger get a pump, or an operation. It is not just how a man makes love or sex for that matter, that a woman stays with him. It's the whole package that matters, or it's also if he wants a committment. Even if a guy is in a partnership, the woman still wants him to committ. In the end a woman wants to stay with a man.

There are some men out there who flirt a lot. Most women say,"Oh he's just being a man". But if a women flirt's she's being fast, a slut, whore, or any other name they can think of. If a women is being nice to a man it is considered flirting. If you take up for a man someone always claims that you like the man. If you give a man a compliment it means that you like him and that's not always the truth. A women can't be nice these days, something always must have a reason behind it. You can't even look at a man without him thinking you like him. A man thinks if he stares with puppy dog eyes that he can get whatever he wants.

There are some men that use religion in a relationship. I know a guy who c laimed he was a baptist, but never went to the church. I know a guy that was muslim, and never went to the mosque. I know a guy that's jehovah witness, and never goes to the temple. To me it doesn't make sense to be involved with a man, if you are not(truelly into) your religion. I know that many people date, or are married that have different religious backgrounds, but they made it through all the hard work of a relationship, or friendship. Again it goes back to what the two people want out of the relationship. There is a pastor I know that says if you are around certain people you will become like them. I know when I was in certain relationships I didn't go to church all the time, once I was in the relationship. The men didn't go and I wanted to be with them so much, I didn't go. The other reason is that when your younger you go so much, Monday bible study, Tuesday c hoir rehearsal, Wednesday Womens' bible study, Thursday Womens' group, Friday Speaker for the week, Saturday bible study, and Sunday church. I feel that I will get into church all the way again when

I am older.  In the mean time I'm still researching the fact if religion is in a relationship, is that a good thing.  I heard one pastor say,"Don't say God brought me this person".  She said that people find people on their own.  There is another pastor that said,"People who do wrong,will never leave you willingly." That's deep ain't it!

There are some men out there who don't seem to care about diseases.  There are a lot of sexual diseases.  There is herpes, syphilus, chlamydia, gonorrhea, aids, and more.  Yes, there are c linics to go to.  There is protection they can use, like condoms and foam.  The foam helps to kill the sperm that may flow from the pre-cum.  Some men don't believe that a women can get pregnant from pre-cum, all it takes is one. There is flavored condoms and dental dam for oral sex.  I feel that now(the present) it's just like the 70's with free love, but it seems like most people are trying to cover it up.  To me, it's like men have no excuse to rape women because of so many women giving up sex so freely.  If you think about it, you may hold out for a good man.  One man comes along with a good job, a car, his own place, and making a good living.  You think he's ok, and after he gets what he wants, be it 2 months or a year or 2, then he lets you down.  He may say he doesn't want a relationship right now.  He may say let's take it slow.  Worst of all he may say,"You're the only one ", while looking for someone else, or someone better than you.

There are some men out there who will give you their cell number, home, and work number. I used to stay with an ex that had a sister and an ex girlfriend with the same name. I remember that I couldn't answer the phone. I figured he had a woman calling the house, or he would have his sister, or aunt call to make me jealous. Anytime a man has a call past ten it's not his mom, it's another woman. I feel a man only wants you to call him at work because he has a wife and kids at home. Some men pick and choose when they want to talk on their cell phone. Either they have a woman their with them, and they won't answer, or they answer and have you to talk quick and to the point. They also won't talk long when their around their boys because either they don't wanna look like their whipped, or their supposed to look like a player. They probably say to their friends,"Oh that's just one of my hoes". I've noticed when I've been around some men they will walk away and then come back when their saying goodbye. An ex of mine called with a girl in the car. He said that the girl was just a friend. I told him,"I bet she doesn't think so." I told him to no longer call me when he has a female in the car. This ex also called me, complaining about women. I asked him had he done anything for them lately. That line from Janet has worked for a long time.

Some men say that most of the time they may not even be worried about another woman. They may just be out trying to get their hustle on, as we say. They also may just want some time to themselves. Some men like to keep to themselves, reading, moping about life and bills, or just watching tv. They also like to spend time with their boys. I know some friends of mine that would stay weekends, or weeks with male friends of theirs. They would go to Reno or Vegas for the weekend. They would also go to visit family for a week in another state. I had a guy to tell me that all he likes to do is travel,then went home with a woman,I guess she pays for him to travel. See they ain't afraid to say what they want.

There are some men who want thier women to look the best that they can, everyday of their life. I know that a woman should look presentable always no matter what. For a woman,hair is costly, whether it's yours or not. We like to have all kinds of styles. The c lothes can cost a lot of money, even if you go to a store that is not as costly. By the time you get through piling things in the basket you've spent a good 200 dollars plus. The shoes cost just as much too because even if you buy the cheapest ones, you buy four or more pairs and there goes the money. I like to dress because it makes me feel good and sexy. I don't dress as often as I used to, so when I do people always ask me do I have a date, or am I going somewhere important. Most of the time I'm just dressing for me to make myself feel better.

Beware of some men who want to know when you get paid. They want to know what you've done for the day to be able to add up how much money you've spent. They may want to know what you've bought so that they can use it too. Once you're not using something anymore, if they can use it they'll ask you for it. Women may also give away things too because they feel sorry for the man. He'll also ask you to pay his bills, his car note, rent, or whatever else. They may feel that since you make more money than them, or that since you take care of your kids, you can help to take care of them too.

Some men decide to change the furniture in the house or in a certain room. I feel they do this, so that when a new woman comes around she won't be able to say,"Oh he had this, this , and this in the house". I know a guy who changed his room once a week. I know a guy that said he bought new furniture, when to me his old furniture was just fine. They add things to the house. You come over they have new computers, new phones, and new cell phones. They can do all this but they c laim that they don't have any money.  Could this be the reason why?

Some men try to c laim that they called you.  You mean to tell me, I have a pager, cell phone, home phone, and a work number, but there was no message.  I love to call guys on it and say, I checked everything and you didn't leave a message, or call.  Why do they lie, is it just because they don't want to tell the truth.  Like for example, I was too busy, or I don't give a shit about you, but ok, you called.  When your with someone you want to know, if they're still ok.  If that accident on the news didn't involve them.  That their not getting into trouble, and just don't want to tell you.  It becomes a mother thing, but they need to realize that friend,or lover, you still care about what they're doing and that they're ok.

Some men try to treat women like hoes(whores).  They give you just enough money to tie you over until you get  paid again.  They call you over late at night.  The one night stand or booty call becomes long term.  They talk to you and treat you any kind of way.  Some men even beat women, they are punks. To me these men are not men, they are boys.  Who gave them the right to treat women this cruel and it's supposed to be ok. They kick you out after the sex.  Some men c laim that they have to go somewhere or they have to go to work, so you'll have to leave. They also may have another women coming over after, or may have had a woman at the house before you were there, think about it!

Oh! Some men only want you over one night of the week. What is that all about? Do they have one woman over each night,Hum?! Why do they only invite you over for Tuesday. Are all the other girls Monday, Wednesday, Thursday, Friday, Saturday, and Sunday is the day to rest. Or, could they be so selfish to where, they do their thang all those days and can only see you one day out of the week. If that's the case they have hella money and they are just keeping it to themselves. They're just stacking it up until they become old and grey. One day, a week, is not enough for most women. If you aren't over your mans' house every day or at least most of the week, somethings wrong. If you guys live together and you don't see him for more than a week, two weeks, or a month somethings wrong.

Some men are too busy doing drugs. There are all kinds out there for them to take. People need to know that c rack and aids really do kill. There are 2 guys that I know that were very close to home that died very recently. They are six feet under, and can't come back. They have inspired me to write this book, and to make my future the greatest it can be. The drugs aren't even noticeable at first. Then the men take more, their tolerance level gets higher. Cocaine is a slow killer. If our people don't control themselves a lot of our race will be gone. The men will not be there to protect, take care, and love their women. Can they blame it on not having a job, no! Make your own business, or get more than one job to make ends meat. There is a way out! Don't just sit there and be lazy, just doing nothing at all, and then expect someone to rescue you. Are we back to slavery days, or what ?!

Some men liked to be called daddy. Is this confusing them? Did they really want to be dad and have a relationship with mom? Is that the quiet secret that's kept? The new word that men use now it's Ma. They may have changed it so that we wouldn't be called man. This is not the past, women are not supposed to be the only bread winners in the family. The only reason women can get jobs is because they don't do drugs and can piss in a cup. There are a lot of men with good jobs. There are a lot of men with ok jobs. Hey Mc, you know who, is hiring. A man should be called daddy only when he is providing all the bread, like back in the day. Other than that, in a relationship both people should earn money, and both should contribute!

There are some men who keep pictures in the house. Most of the time it is pictures of their women, her or his kids, or other family members. If the pictures don't go away, or have not been moved the next time you visit most likely she is still around. If they try to play it off like it doesn't mean nothing, it does. If they have only one or more it still means that they're together. Oh yeah, and they may even say that it's a sister, cousin, or just someone that they took a picture with. This should tell you if the guy is a player because he will have pictures of more than one woman.

There are some men who will talk about their woman like a dog. They do this because they want you to think that they hate her, and can't get along with her. I feel they want you to think that if he hates her then he will leave her, or that you can make him feel better, or treat him better than she does. All that I can take care of you better is true in some ways, in some ways not. All woman may have the same thing. A man can get anywhere he chooses to. A man that I know said that he could date women from 21 to 85. He is exaggerating, but it's true. A man will choose which woman he wants to spend his life with. He will choose if he wants to marry a woman or not. At the time that a man is telling you he hates his woman they may be going through problems but he may never leave her. Most of the time it is the woman that leaves. Don't get me wrong, the men cut out too. Either a woman can choose to stay with the man and put up with all his shit or she can choose to go about her own way, Next!!!

There are some men who will talk to you and sweet talk you down. Then it will be a few days or a week and their woman will call and say that thier married. Then they'll call you back and say that the woman was lying. Over the years I have had quite a few women that have called to say that they're men are already taken. I've had some to ask me how and where did I meet the guy. I've had women to ask me why. I always tell them that's just the way they are. I don't like it, they either don't know any better, they don't know that they have a good woman, or they are just a player! trying to get some snatch,puntang!!

There are some men who claim their from out of town. They say that their usually from another state and that they just got here. When they know that they are from right here in Oakland. They also say that they'll only be in town for a little while and that you can only see them for just a few days or something like that. Of course this is only part of the game. He wants you to think that if you don't go to bed with him real soon that you'll miss something that you've never had. When the truth is that he lives right in your hood. They know that their lieing only to get you in bed. I'm sure that some women fall for it. I'm sure that some women think that they can use them for a while, but again their only looking for one extra thing because they probably have a few women already.  And if a player doesn't want you, it because you ain't his type, or he's ignoring you to pull you in later.

Some men, when you are at their house, will not let you answer their phone.  I don't like answering the phone anyway because of some woman calling, that thier trying to play with. Your in his house and the phone rings at midnight, come on now, you know it's a booty call.  If a call comes in the day time, for that matter, it's probably a woman either trying to see if he's at home, or she's telling him she's at home, or that she made it home from work.  I had an experience where I used to answer the phone just to see if it was another woman, it wasn't, but he could have had them call to work or another number.

Some men don't like it when you drop by their house without calling first.  I hate this comment with a passion.  They say that a woman thinks that they are cheating and that's why she does it.  My friends say he ain't shit because he has you calling first.  I say the only reason that I do it is that I should be able to.  A man will tell you, your the only one, that you should trust him. Then your girls tell you, you should be able to go over anytime you want.  I had a man that would come over to my house without calling and I didn't like it.  I told him to call first.

I feel, to each her or his own. They also try to say that if you call first, but they don't talk to you, then you aren't supposed to come by. You aren't supposed to come by because he has someone else there.

Some men don't want their women to get pregnant. They may feel that they can't afford a baby. They may feel that since your not married that a woman shouldn't have a baby. This is the reason why some men beat their women. They may also have another woman, or other women, so they don't want a baby. They get mad at her having it, they can't take care of themselves and a baby. This is also why some men leave, or quit the relationship with a woman. They don't care or think about the future of the child, or the mother.All they care about is themselves.

Some men want women to get pregnant. They want a child to have their name. They also want to teach them how to be a player, if it's a boy. If it's a girl they say that no guy will be able to touch her. They want to get a woman pregnant so they can have some rest of their life puntang. I was told by a man that his uncle told him all he had to do was get a woman pregnant and he was set for life. I've known a lot of guys who have created baby's mamas. All they do is spend a few months to a year. Then they treat them any kind of way.

Some wait until the baby is born, then they end the relationship. Some men will make it an on-off thang, where they'll see you for six months,and then 2 weeks in a month after that. That's why when a man asks you is the dad still around and you say yes, they immediately think your going to be with him still. I struggled for 2 years with that situation until I finally let go. I finally got to where I don't even speak to him.

Some men always stay together as roommates. It can be two or three that stay together in one place. The man that you meet like this will probably never change. He will go from one roommate to two. He may even ask you to move in, but believe you me, it's to buy the groceries, pay rent, or whatever else they need. They will try to claim that they don't have much money because they pay rent and bills even though there are two people in the home. He may even say that he's the only one paying the bills because his roommate couldn't come up with the money. Oh yeah, don't forget the car note and whatever else. Oh yes, I also heard from another woman, do not mess with musicians because they don't ever have money because their paying for their equipment. I know , I am an R and B Artist. I pay for studio time and I know how much equipment costs because I want to a studio in my home, but

I still have money left over to go to the movies, or treat myself to dinner, or shop.

There are some men who totally flip the scrip, as we say. A guy will be with you for a few months to a year and all of a sudden he doesn't call, or come by any more. You will see him, or your family will see him, and he's doing just fine but he's not calling you. You may even go by the house yourself and even see him, but he'll talk to you for a second or just tell you he'll call. You spend all that time together trying to go through hard times, or going through ups and downs and he just brushes you off. There's got to be either someone else, or something that he's going through.

There are some men who will let you go with no problem. Women need to let you go with no problem. Women need to let go and go on with their lives. When a man dec- ides to let a woman go it's cut and dry. They may tell you flat out no when you want a kiss, sex, or definitely help. Their heart is turned off and believe you me, it will not change for a long time, or not at all. They don't care how they tell you off, or no. They don't care about your feelings. It hurts so bad to be rejected. As long as you give it to them, or help them out everything is fine but when their finished with you, their done, and out for the count.

There are some men who live off of women.  Don't get me wrong they still may have their hustle, but the women may work and have good money.  The guy may turn around and lose his job.  Then the woman treats him just like a big baby.  He may take care of the kids, or not.  No matter what a man should be a man.  You know there is a place called MCDonalds.  There are other jobs that may not pay much, retail, but it can do the job.  The woman may also be waiting for the man to get himself together, but when they get to a certain age they only have so long to go.  Do they think about retirement?  Do they even care?

There are som men who take advantage of a good woman.  They don't know what they have, until it's gone.  There are a lot of good women out there who want a good man and want to get married.  Maybe the men want to run away when it comes to marriage.  There are are some men who want to get married but I guess some way, you can meet your soul mate.  A woman with a good job, can cook and c lean, has good conversation, good morals, and intelligence, I guess for some men is not enough.  Some women don't even go out and get other men.  A woman that rejects other men and keeps to herself, I guess is not good enough either.  I still feel that for most men it's seeing their past and how their father beat their

34

mother. Maybe their parents fought every night. They may have even had a single parent and don't believe in marriage. Most men tell women what they want to hear. They should tell a woman up front that they don't want to get married. That'd be too much like right.

There are some men that don't know what they're doing. They don't know how to get legal work. They don't know how to go to college. They don't know how to get a job. They don't know how to carry themselves. They don't know how to take care of themselves. Women don't have the upper hand just by twiddling their thumbs and sitting on their ass. Women get out there and work, and talk for theirs. We go to college to better ourselves. When we're at work people get to us but we don't quit. The boss may be on our back but we go past that and deal with it. We may cry when bills come,most don't, but we find out how to pay them. If we don't know something we read. Reading is knowledge!

and power!! Also you can ask anyone questions that you have, and most people will help you.

I just had to add this part, kids are not stupid. They can see your man with someone else, and they will tell you. They may hear you talking on the phone about your relationship and they will tell you exactly what they think, and you better listen because they will tell you how to take care of your situation. I've experienced kids saying how a guy talked to another woman. They'll tell you if your not with the guy anymore, if they saw him. Kids aint stupid! Pay attention to them, they're amazing. Most people try to hide their relationships from their kids but in some moments they are there , and they'll let you know how they feel.

Let me be real and spit a true part of the game. Some players cheat right in front of other women that they know. I'm gonna tell the truth and I hope it doesn't hurt, I have seen men that I know with other women that I don't know. I know that the women they are with are friends, and some are not. Some friends you don't tell what he's doing not because he's a true player but because you don't want to hurt their feelings. Some men you'll tell the woman about to warn her. Even I ran into that one and the guy turned around and dogged me too. Whoof!Whoof! I feel that women should tell each other which man, or men they are trippin', or in a relationship with. I've told some guy friends what their women have said so they wouldn't get played. All I'm trying to say is that if your man is a player he will play with you, or without you! So keep your eyes open, and make the right decisions. If not learn and make yourself stronger by your mistakes.

There are some men who think while your with them you should still have friends on the side. I feel that if a man wants you to have friends on the side, he doesn't want you. They try to say that it's ok for you to have other friends because your not married, but that is not true. They don't really want a relationship, they just want you as one of their females. They want you to hang with them , and for you to be dangling on a string until they get ready to do whatever they want to you.

There are some men who will take advantage of young girls. These young girls will have the babies and will not ba able to take care of them on their own. The men know it, and try to get the girl to have sex so they can get money to feed the kids. The girls may also be into drugs and the men may take advantage of them. The young girl may be looking for love in all the wrong places, and they need to find another way to find it.

There are some men out there that molest or rape young women. I know lots of women who have been molested by a family member. I have had this happen to me and my father(known as a friend to the family) was not charged. He wasn't even taken to court because he was helping mom with money for the house. I have talked to many women where their uncle, cousin, friend of the family, neighbor, or mothers boyfriend molested them. I know when I was a teenager, there was a girl who asked for help with some money from my best friend and I. She said that her moms' boyfriend had raped her, but that her mom had kicked her out the house, and she had nowhere else to go. I also knew a woman where she was raped by her friends father because she liked his daughter. The girl didn't change to liking men, she still liked women, and is a great person. There are thousands of these stories out there.

There are some men who think just because they say,"Hey come here," that you will call or talk to him. Your friends think that you know the guy, but you don't. I myself, I try not to be rude, but I know that it makes me look like I'm being a ho. To me that's not fair, It makes the women look cheap and easy when she may not be that way. If you don't respond, I know one guy said,"Bitch", just because I didn't say nothing to him.

Some men want you to sell your body. They know that you may be fast and with this guy or that guy. They ask if you need money and they want sex in return. They may say,"I'll pay your bills, but I want something in return." Don't get me wrong, I call it the under prostitution. Your not on the street, your in your home, they know that you can't pay your bills, your going hungry, your just plain poor. Then they try to take advantage of that by giving you money in your hand and they undress you, and physically have sex with you.

There are some men out there who will only call you their friend because you are not married. Even if you are girlfriend and boyfriend, or a player and one of his unsuspecting women, no matter which friends you are around he will always introduce you as his friend. This has always urked me, but unless your married this will never change. They also callyou a friend because they don't plan on ever marrying you. A friend of mine says it takes a while to think about marrying somone,Damn how long is long!

It is a very, very, very small world. Every player, man, or beast that you know, you will see again in life. You can bet on it, even if things are going great for you. You will most likely see someone that you know from your past, more than 5 or 6 times again in your life, if not more. You also don't know, who they know, that you know. You could be at a new job and you could see them. Make sure that you are careful about the men and people you are around in your lifetime.

There are some men out there who do not pay child support. They will lie out the back of their teeth, saying that they take care for their children. You don't see them helping them. You don't see them mailing off the envelope of money.

You don't see the order of support saying how much they pay per month. You don't talk to the other baby's mama to see how much she gets. You may not talk to the other woman at all, because he may still be sleeping with her. You don't know exactly how many women he really has. He may have 9 kids that you or he won't know about. On top of that he may say, and the baby's mama may say, that it's none of your business. It is if your giving that nigga money to take care of himselfand them kids.

There are some men out there that are very dangerous. I call them, more than perverts. They will treat you all kinds of ways. They will make you do some things sexually that you probably would never do if a friend or a family member knew what you were doing. When they look at you they stare you down like your a piece of meat. They look at you in a terrible way becaue they want to have sex with you. They will talk to you about your relationhips, sex, anything with no problem. I hate talking to men, your friendly to them then after a few months or years they feel they can talk sexually toward you, it's degrading.

There are some men who will take you to court in a minute. They are either hoping to get their children or they are just being mean to get a woman back for leaving them.

They will do whatever they have to, to get the child in their custody. You better have a good lawyer. You better have all your information ready for the judge to hear. If a blood

test will make the situation end, do it. I was in a situation, I listened to my lawyer instead of doing what I wanted which was the blood test. My situation would have been cleared after that. I also thought that the father was the father so I didn't push the issue. I look at everything fully now. My mom told me from the jump to give the boys my last name. Damn, I should've listened, mothers always know best. If you ask them anything, listen and use the advice.

There are some men out there that do not want to be seen with you. They may take you to only see some friends. You can only meet some family members. They will only go with you to a c ertain mall and not others because their other women probably shop at the other malls. You can only got to certain movie places and if you ask them you are paying. Your better off going by yourself. They only take you to certain bar b ques, and you must buy the food because you and your children need to eat. They only take you to certain clubs, if you see them with another woman, some women confront them, and most don't. After that we just don't have anything to do with them. If he is only taking you out once a week then the other women are taken out on the other days.

There are some men that say they have been to college. They say they've been to other states. They say they are divorced. Whatever they have done make sure that you have seen the papers. They could lie until the c ows come home, and you wouldn't know anything about it. I have been told by so many men that they are divorced or their wife left them and there are c lothes still in the closet. The guys that have been to college, i never saw any transcripts.

There are some men that you meet in the c lub. People always say don't meet anyone in a c lub. They say that the women are really fast in the c lub. I've been to the c l- ub and heard women say that their man was messing around so they will find someone for the night. I know some men that will talk about every women they've been with. They talk about them so bad it's ridiculous. If the women knew how they talked about them, they wouldn't be bothered.

There are some men that are younger and are serious players. They will lay down with anything to get whatever they want or need. They treat women like ho's. They're the ho's. They will f--- anything and everything, and even without a rubber(condom). There are men that are older and are players.

They will take you one place. They still treat women like ho's. They will deal with them until the woman has an attitude, or won't give him any money anymore. The guys that I've talked to over the years say that older men will treat you better. I know from experience that even the older ones are mostly still out for some tail(sex).

There are some men that will not call you at all nowadays. You can call them until your hair turns grey, but they will not call you no matter what. They don't call because they know you'll call no matter what. You'll wonder what their doing all the time. They probably also think that this way you'll stay in the house waiting for your call. They may not even give a shit, what your doing, they're just doing what they gotta do, and don't care about you.

There are some men out there that don't have any goals in life. They like where their at, and what they're doing so they don't strive for anything more. They don't care about being smarter. They don't care about being productive. They don't care about their future. They don't care about being richer. They just want to be in the position or situation that their in, and complain about being poor, or not having any money. They don't say ok in 3 months I want to have this job. In 6 months I want to have this job. In 1 year I want to be president of my own

43

company. We all must have goals in life to get anywhere. This is the only way to improve your happiness, and your lifestyle.

There are somen men who are players that are in the church. I have run across some players that will be with one girl one month, and a new girl the next month. I have heard guys talk about the main reason they go to church is to see all the girls. There are some men that havebeen deacons or preachers that I heard had gotten a few girls pregnant. That's why it's important for some teenagers to learn about safe sex. I know about a situation where a girl that comes to a church and sits with the same guy. Another girl said that the guy told her he was single. They had gone to dinner, and then the girl who sits with him admits that he is a ho' and they were supposed to get married.

There are some men out there that teach their younger brothers, cousins, or friends how to be players. These young players even try to talk to older women. They try to play the younger girls like a merry-go-round. One little guy has the nerve to have supposedly six girls that liike him. I hear stories all the time about young women sleeping around like it's the thing to do. These boys have even tried to flirt with me and I tell them,"Boy I'm old enough to be your mama." What I don't tell them is if they were my son I would beat there butt. To me, young men don't even know half of what the older players know, and most likely their not even ready for sex. Yeah, they may say,"Oh,You don't know how much I know,"But I know things that they don't know, and it's a lot.

There are some men out there that will propose to a woman. To me, most of them are just not ready for a real comittment. I feel that some men also use proposing just to hold onto a woman. To me they feel that there may not be a better woman out there for them. I was proposed to 4 times in my life. The first time I felt we weren't ready. The next three the men weren't ready. I don't believe in no long term relationship, like 5 or 10 years to get married either. After 2 years, to me, it should be enough time for the couple to tell if they can be compatible enough to be together. I've talked to a lot of women and men where the marraiges didn't work out, but there are a lot that have.

There are some men out there that will cook for you, play music, listen to you, or whatever your heart desires. I have talked to a lot of men that say that music is the way to a womans' bed. Some men have actual sex tapes, I call it. It's music to make a woman melt. It's all the songs for even a certain age group, that she will make love to after listening to it. Whether the men can sing or not, it still works like a charm.

They will listen to you if you talk a lot(like me), or a little. This means that he is paying attention to everything that you say. It makes the woman feel like, "Oh, he cares about me." He may not even give a shit, it still may be just so he can get into the panties. Some may buy you c lothes, they may buy you jewelry, flowers, or candy. They may give you everything your heart desires, but it may be all done just to get you in the bed. I've been given c lothes, jewelry, perfume, cooked for, and I still feel it was all done to get me in the bed.

There are some players that will take you on trips. They will take you to Reno or Las Vegas. They may take you out of state, or on a cruise but it's just to get you in the bed. I have seen men invite women on c ruises one week and then talk about them in between. As soon as you aee the women again she talks about how their going on another c ruise together. That's why when I hear a guy say that their going to Reno or Vegas I kind of smile. I always wanna ask are you taking a female with you? There is a guy I know that only goes on trips when his female gives him the money. I know guys that only go on trips, because the women that they're with at the moment, is paying and has asked him to go with her. There are some guys that I know where their woman pays for them to go on a trip!Ain't that a bitch!

There are some men who will show you letters from the last women he was with! Warning! Warning! Warning! This is a very strong sign that he is a no good individual. Most likely he has played the other woman, or is still with the other woman and you are the one on the side, especially if he has more than one. There is some kind of drama going on with him and you should not deal with it right away. Nowadays they try to say that a woman is c razy and that's why they don't live or deal with them anymore, but to me they are the ones that are unstable and should get help real soon. If you see hate letters, good letters, any kind from another female, GET OUT!

There are some men that lie about when their gonna be home and what they are doing. I say always check up on a player. People say if you can't trust someone, it's really true, you shouldn't be with them. A guy can fuss at you and say if you don't trust me we shouldn't be together, no you shouldn't. Most likely there are a lot of signs that you are not paying attention to. Sex toys, porno flicks, womens names on the phone bill or fax machine, any kind of sign to say that he is no good. There can be c lothes, shoes, anything from a woman that wasn't there before and no it's not mamas'. It's a harsh truth to face but face it right away, don't just keep letting things happen.

There are some men who try to enroll their kids into schools without you even knowing. They may even try to get the women that their with to do it. This experience happened to me, if I hadn't have been moving to the city, I don't know what would've happened. You always have to fight about what you want to do, as far as even, if your going to put the child in school or not. I feel it is really wrong for a guy to try to convince you where to send your child to school.

There are some men out there who want to take over, and take care of your kid. It may be because he needs a welfare check, wants to keep the child to his self or his mate, the main reason is so that they don't have to pay child support. They also may be on drugs and they need to supply their habit. They feel that they can take care of the child. Children are a handful at 0-1 years, terrible 2's, treacherous 3's, up to teen age, at teenage their really a handful and after that you need to try to send them on their way. Children are a blessing, but they are a handful, and you must raise their right or their adulthood will be spent in jail.

There are some men out there who don't pay child support for their kids. they will not pay because they figure that the child isn't theirs. Most people say that even if the child isn't the guys he should still pay child support if he's known the child ever since the baby was born. I was in a situation like this. I thought the ex that I was with was my sons father, forever. I was only with one other guy. We had a blood test done, I was shocked and hurt that he wasn't the father. I was not trying to trap him, I just really didn't know, or because of the due date, I really, really thought he was the father. Now I see how players are and I finally got tired of it. If I knew then what I know now I would have given my son my last name. The situation would have been taken care of and the ex could have gone on with his life.

There are some men who think that a woman is supposed to be other peoples' property. Some men tell their friends I had it ,you can have it now. Most women do not want to be other peoples' property. I know that most women want to be honored and protected by being married. Most women do not want to deal with all of the bullshit it takes to stay with a player. Some men will tell you that their woman is ok with them seeing other women on the side. Some men will say that what their women don't Inow won't hurt, but I still say, if he knew he would get cursed out, or left. There are some men that don't care if they get left, but those are the ones who were probably no good from the jump.

There are some men who will flirt to no end. Most people say all men flirt, it's just their way. I feel there should be a limit to the flirting. There's a difference between being a flirt and being a gentlemen, and being a flirt and being nasty. I feel that some men get more gross when their drinking. Some men get more gross just because they think they can. Just because a women smiles or laughs when a guy says something gross doesn't mean that she likes what he is saying. We just don't slap men like they did back in the day, but I feel this should change because it's very disrespectful to women. Some men might say that some women like it but it's a lie. I know for a fact most women don't because as soon as the guy turns around they really say what they feel about his gross ass. He's thinking that he is the biggest player on earth and smiling as he walks away!

You know it really pisses me off when some men out there think that by buying a women a drink, they get the gratitude of having sex. I hate to be a bitch, but you think because you've bought a 4 dollar drink that a women is gonna give you sex, COME ON NOW! Even if a guy bought 2 or 6 drinks there should be no expectation of going home, but they make you feel like it though. I know a lot of guys may have had some women who have done that, but what has she been through. Did her man leave her?, Is she just fast?, Is she young and dumb?, or old and dumb for that matter?! These sayings have been used for ump-teen years and I still feel that no one knows a womans true story and what they may have been through,until they talk to her. Be very careful about alcohol being used for sexual reasons!!! They say that alcohol dilutes a womans thinking. She can not think straight once the alcohol kicks in so they make the wrong decision so be careful! On a very popular show(Oprah) statistics say that 1-2 drinks are .8,3-4 drinks are.16, 6-7 drinks is bing drinking, can give you seizures,and you can black out. I know that my friend and I drove around looking for a guy,she doesn't drink as much as I have, and to me thirty minutes was like two hours. Alcohol slows down your mental capabilities,you'll be surprised how much.

There are some men who will ignore you once you have done anything to give them the wrong idea, kissing them, flirting with them, even just letting them know that you like them. You know I have to say there are some women who think this is the thing to do. I think it can be dangerous at times, and they should be careful. They may ignore you because they want someone to look at them as a player. They may try to act like they don't know you because their busy flirting with other women. They may have done it because they just want to keep coming around to see you. They can just be down right rude and it's how they feel about getting whatever kind of person they want. On top of that they can just think that they look that damn good to ignore you and any other woman they deal with. All that fine or whatever else, ain't worth it!

There are some that will put your picture up everytime you come by, Does it mean anything? Well it depends on the player. He could take it down when your not there, or leave it up for some other woman to see. It is a trip though to know that your only there sometime, say once a week, and your pictures still in the same exact place. It makes you want to make a mark on the table, door, or dresser where ever it is to make sure that it hasn't been moved within the last week. Some women may not even worry about stuff like that, but if you've got a player, you'd wanna think about it!!

# Conclusion

There are places to get information on safe sex information or situations that you must deal with in being involved with the opposite sex like planned parenthood or other clinics that you can look up in the telephone book. There are magazines that you can read on relationships like Oprah, Essence, or other magazines that you may be interested in. There are talk shows on relationships like Jennie Jones, (which I've Been On), Ricky Lake, Montell, Dr. Phil, and many other shows that deal with people in relationships, marriage, and dating. I feel that when it comes to Black Historysome people should look at the books of the past like autobiographies of Martin Luther King,Malcolm X, Frederick Douglas, WEB Dubois, Rosa Parks, Ruby Bridges, Maya Angelo, Mary McCloud Bethune,(Whom I Admired all my life), Arthur Ashe(Whom I read about in my junior high library), Nat Turner, George Washington Carver, and many more of our Black Role Models.

There is one thing that I would like to see change is Black History Month, I know in the school system it lasts it seems for just a few days. the children don't get to see Roots, and movies on the civil rights movement. I feel that Black children should have more role models so that they can have something to look up to. Yes, there are future stars out there, but if the children new where we came from and could be proud of who we are it would be a joy. I feel that anyone and everyone should take the time to go to the library. It would be so rewarding to do this. The library has books for people to read, computers to use, and it depends on which library it is they have activities for the kids. Every other nationality lives together, helps each other to get jobs, and helps families to stay together financially. With our people we are so busy trying to do for ourselves that we can't get together. My mom told me how back in the day, the Black Families were the ones that had the businesses. Now it seems to me that every other nationality are the main ones with the businesses, or is it just me?! The teachers in the school system are not the only ones that can teach the children. It starts with the parents. You can only do as much as you can. *It is amazing what can happen from baby to teenager. Where are all the middle class Blacks, or rich for that matter? Is world about to become the poor being the poor, and the rich being the rich? Is the younger generation going to always keep going faster than the next? Where are Blacks going to be in the future? Will we rise to the top and take our place up front where we should be like everyone else? Will our women always be the last choice for a man? The Black woman is at the bottom of the barrel when it comes to wife potential. I feel that men look for white, then Asian, or any other nationality. Then they use Black woman until they get to the piece of the pie? Are my questions to straight and to the point? Well I just want people to think deep about what their doing to our race and our women in general,(especially them). It is time for the* world to hear the secrets that men don't want you to know or believe because their game will be exposed!!!

*Thank you Very Much For Reading My Book,*

*Traci*

# About the Author

She is a single mother with a bachelor's degree in liberal studies. She has told stories all of her life and finally put her foot down to tell her story. For years she has written stories and listened to her community. She has heard lots of different issues and situations, but she is here to tell her story.

www.ingramcontent.com/pod-product-compliance
Lightning Source LLC
Chambersburg PA
CBHW020354290526
45785CB00005B/2274